The PRAYER *of* JABEZ *for* WOMEN

THE BREAKTHROUGH SERIES

THE
PRAYER *of* JABEZ
for Women

BREAKING THROUGH *to the*
BLESSED LIFE

DARLENE WILKINSON

Multnomah®Publishers *Sisters, Oregon*

THE PRAYER OF JABEZ FOR WOMEN
published by Multnomah Publishers, Inc.

© 2002 by Darlene Wilkinson

International Standard Book Number: 1-57673-962-7

Cover design by David Carlson Design

Cover image by Shotwell & Associates, Inc.

Scripture is from *The Holy Bible,* New King James Version (NKJV)
Copyright © 1982 by Thomas Nelson, Inc. Used by permission.

Other Scripture quotations:
New American Standard Bible (NASB)
© 1960, 1977 by the Lockman Foundation

Multnomah is a trademark of Multnomah Publishers, Inc.,
and is registered in the U.S. Patent and Trademark Office.
The colophon is a trademark of Multnomah Publishers, Inc.

Printed in the United States of America

For information:
MULTNOMAH PUBLISHERS, INC.
POST OFFICE BOX 1720
SISTERS, OREGON 97759

Library of Congress Cataloging-in-Publication Data

Wilkinson, Darlene
    The prayer of Jabez for women / by Darlene Wilkinson.
        p. cm.
    ISBN 1-57673-962-7 (hardcover)
    1. Bible. O.T. Chronicles, 1st, IV, 10--Prayers--History and criticism. 2. Christian
women--Religious life. 3. Jabez (Biblical figure). 4. Prayer--Christianity. I. Title.
    BS1345.6.P68 W56 2002
    248.8'43--dc21

02 03 04 05 06 07 08—10 9 8 7 6 5 4 3 2 1 0

WHAT A PRIVILEGE TO DEDICATE THIS BOOK
TO FIVE VERY SPECIAL WOMEN IN MY LIFE:

my mother, Susie
my mother-in-law, Joan
my daughters, Jennifer and Jessica
my daughter-in-law, Angie

THANK YOU FOR BEING A BLESSING TO ME.

∾ *Acknowledgments* ∾

Behind every book are the smiling faces of those who contributed to make it all possible. I want to say a special thank-you:

To my gifted editor and friend Heather Harpham Kopp, whose gracious guidance and invaluable instruction made the writing process such a delight.

To the Walk Thru the Bible Prayer Team and Prayer Committee for their love and support in praying the prayer of Jabez and seeing God expand borders.

To Anne Ortman, Dorit Radandt, and Janis Simmons for the enjoyable hours of brainstorming together.

To the many friends that made suggestions, shared their stories, and offered their time so this book could reach the finish line.

To my loving family, who prayed for me, cheered me on, and remained understanding so deadlines could be met.

To my wonderful husband and best friend, Bruce, whose inspiration and unconditional love motivated me to reach for my dream.

And most of all to my incredible God, whose loving-kindness and tender mercies bless me, indeed!

Table of Contents

~ Darlene's Letter to You ~

If you're like me, at some point or another you've probably looked down the road you're traveling and thought, *Is this all there is, or is there more to this journey through life than I'm currently experiencing?*

That's a great question.

And the little prayer I want to introduce you to can help you find the answer. It's only one sentence with four parts, and it is located in an obscure part of the Bible. But I believe that it contains a powerful secret that has the potential to change your journey from ordinary to extraordinary. Of course, it was never meant to be a "secret," but then, isn't everything a secret to us until we discover it?

I believe that God wants you to find out for yourself what is so amazing about these four requests made by a man named Jabez. In fact, you are an answer to my prayer that God would deliver this message into the hands and hearts of millions of women around the world. Won't you join me on the journey of a lifetime?

I am praying you will!

Darlene

CHAPTER ONE

Made for More

 very summer I look forward to attending our town's annual Fourth of July parade. This year the weather is perfect—sunny and warm with a light breeze. Hundreds of people line the streets, which are abuzz with anticipation. I maneuver myself for a better position in the crowd as our local high school band rounds the corner. The sound of trumpets reaches my ears. Finally, horses, clowns, and floats come into view.

That's when I notice her—a little girl with curly blond hair just a few feet to my right. She is standing on her tiptoes, stretching her small frame as high as she can to see over the heads of the children in front of her. Moments later, an extra-wide man moves in front of the girl, and she's left looking at the back of his belt. As I watch, she begins to jump up and down, desperately trying to catch a better view.

She is standing on her tiptoes, stretching her small frame as high as she can.

II

Finally, unable to handle her frustration any longer, she cries out, "I can't see, Daddy! I want to see more."

A tall, nice-looking man who has been standing a short distance away comes over, reaches down, and tenderly lifts her up into his arms. She smiles with delight. Finally she's able to fully enjoy the parade.

That's the picture that comes to mind when I think about what happens when God knows I am "stretching for a better view" of my life. It's as if He picks me up in His loving arms and shows me something I couldn't see from my current or limited perspective.

He has a special plan to abundantly bless you and then bless others through you.

The powerful little prayer I'm about to share with you is also about seeing things from a new vantage point. I believe that God brought you to this book because He wants to show you something surprising and amazing about His intentions for you. He has a special plan to abundantly bless you and then bless others through you—and He doesn't want you to miss out on a minute of it!

A CHANGE OF HEART

The first time I heard about the prayer of Jabez, I didn't really give it much thought. At the time I was busy working on my Ph.T. degree (putting hubby through school). After seminary, Bruce took a teaching position, and I became a stay-at-home mom with our first two children, David and Jennifer. I loved my role as wife and mother and was enjoying my dream come true.

But then it happened. The endless list of things to do to raise a family, run a household, and be the wife of a traveling husband convinced me of the truth of the statement "A woman's work is never done." Don't misunderstand, some days I felt like the richest woman in the world. But other days left me thinking something I never thought I would think: *I was made for more than this.*

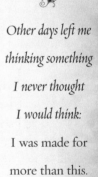

Other days left me thinking something I never thought I would think: I was made for more than this.

Meanwhile, Bruce would come home from teaching school or giving Walk Thru the Bible seminars and tell me about all the exciting things God was doing in his life. I, on the other hand, could give an account of how many Cheerios I had picked up off the floor, how many loads of clothes I had folded, and how many books I had reread to the children. It wasn't hard to decide who had the more significant life—or so I thought.

Until then I had considered the prayer of Jabez something

that might as well be labeled "For Men Only." After all, Jabez himself was a man, and in addition to my husband, most of the people I knew who prayed the prayer were men.

Now I began to wonder, *Is it possible? Could the prayer of a herdsman who lived thousands of years ago bring blessing and abundance to a woman's life today? If so, what might that look like?*

Spurred on by the exciting stories I heard from Bruce and others who prayed this prayer, I began to use the words of Jabez to express the deepest longings of my own heart. I pleaded with God for a better and bigger view of my life, one that would reveal what He had in mind for me.

Ever so gently, God began to challenge some of my earlier conclusions. Could it be that my world wasn't as limited as I sometimes deemed it? Was I missing important opportunities right in front of me to see God at work? Might it even be true that I *was* born for more and God was now inviting me to experience something grand and significant that I had overlooked?

Each time I prayed the prayer of Jabez, I had more understanding about what I was really asking God to do. Soon I began seeing His character, my own life, and the circumstances around me in a new light. God's blessings began to flow into my life and, even better, to flow in obvious ways from me into the lives of others! I wanted to keep praying the prayer because God kept answering it.

WHY JABEZ FOR WOMEN?

As you may already be aware, God is using the prayer of Jabez to change millions of lives. Men, women, and teens have responded to the message and embarked on the Jabez journey. So why write a Jabez book especially for women?

At first I wasn't sure there was a need. After all, the message of Jabez is already aimed at both men and women. But as women all over the world began to write letters to Bruce in response to Jabez, I noticed that they raised questions and talked about issues that were important and wholly unique to women. I observed that God is equally excited to answer this prayer for both men and women but that we experience those answers in very different ways.

Soon I began seeing His character, my own life, and the circumstances around me in a new light.

This only makes sense. As women, we do face different challenges than men. We experience different kinds of temptations, and we look for different kinds of help and provision from God's hand. Many of us are caretakers and spend a great deal of time nurturing our families and friends. As a result, we approach ministry and relationships differently than men.

Jabez's ancient, simple prayer is surprisingly suited to the modern-day woman.

For these reasons and more, there's much to be gained by looking at what happens when we pray the prayer of Jabez *as women*.

I don't promise that you'll find every answer for every woman in this book, but I will try to help you understand what it means to live out Jabez's life *as a woman*. By the time you're done reading, I trust you'll agree with me that Jabez's ancient, simple prayer is surprisingly suited to the modern-day woman who longs for God's powerful touch on her life.

THE BIBLE'S HIDDEN HERO

If this is the first time you've been introduced to the prayer of Jabez, you may be saying to yourself, *I've heard of Moses, David, and John the Baptist, but who in the world is Jabez?*

Remember when you first decided to read 1 Chronicles? Chapter 1 begins with a genealogy dating back to Adam that lasts nine chapters. You may have enjoyed exercising your phonics skills on the more than five hundred names like

Shephatish or Aholibamah. But my guess is that by the second chapter of names that were difficult to pronounce, you were skimming through the verses, trying to find where the story begins. Oops, that may be how you missed Jabez, who doesn't appear until chapter 4.

Hidden in the midst of Israel's family tree is the story of a man who'd been standing on his tiptoes, trying to see over the obstacles in front of him. Two short verses give us a brief look at this man and how he prayed:

> Now Jabez was more honorable than his brothers, and his mother called his name Jabez, saying, "Because I bore him in pain." And Jabez called on the God of Israel saying, "Oh, that You would bless me indeed, and enlarge my territory, that Your hand would be with me, and that You would keep me from evil, that I may not cause pain!" So God granted him what he requested. (1 Chronicles 4:9–10, NKJV)

Did you notice that Jabez is not heralded in the Scriptures for his incredible talents or gifts? Nothing is mentioned about how he contributed or what he accomplished. God points out that he was "more honorable." That should encourage us, because honor and integrity are qualities that any of us can strive to achieve. When we do, God is much more inclined to hear and answer our prayers just as He did for Jabez.

By now you also may be wondering: *Did God grant Jabez's requests* only *because he was honorable? Or was there something special about what he prayed?*

That's a good question. Since God considered Jabez "honorable" and then chose to include his prayer in the Bible, we can be sure that He considered it a noteworthy example for us to follow. But that's not the only reason Jabez's prayer is effective. As you're about to discover, though Jabez lived and prayed thousands of years before the time of Jesus, his prayer is a wonderful example of how Jesus taught us to pray.

God points out that Jabez was "more honorable."

Let's take a look at the four key parts to Jabez's prayer:

Oh, that You would bless me indeed,
and enlarge my territory,
that Your hand would be with me,
and that You would keep me from evil.
(1 Chronicles 4:10, NKJV)

Maybe at first glance these appear to be four very simple, even unremarkable, requests. But let me assure you that hidden beneath each line is a biblical and life-changing principle of prayer.

The prayer of Jabez is not a magic formula, nor should it be the only prayer you pray. Yet as we look more closely at each of Jabez's requests, you'll discover why God loves to answer such a prayer. And you'll understand why praying it can release the miraculous in your life.

WHEN GOD LEANS DOWN

Did I just say "miraculous"?

Yes, I did! Wouldn't it be great to go from a life in which the mundane—appointments, chores, carpools—seems to rule to a life in which you see miracles taking place on a regular basis? Wouldn't you love to see things happening in your life that you knew were possible only because God leaned down and said "yes" to something you prayed for?

My friend Peggy says she'd all but given up on the idea of miracles taking place in her life. Then she began praying the prayer of Jabez—and God began answering in amazing ways. One of the most exciting involved a restored relationship. "I had given up hope years ago that my

The prayer of Jabez is not a magic formula, nor should it be the only prayer you pray.

estranged sister, Jessie, would ever darken the door of my home again," she explains. "But I'd been praying the prayer of Jabez for only a few days when I received a tearful phone call from Jessie! She asked my forgiveness for past wrongs and told me she wanted to be sisters again." She adds, "If you knew our family's history, you'd understand what a huge miracle this was!"

"God truly wants me to ask in faith for His generous blessings."

Maybe the idea of these kinds of miracles sounds a little intimidating to you. Or perhaps it's the idea of asking for "more" in your life that sounds overwhelming.

That's what Dianne thought when she first read *The Prayer of Jabez*. Busy with a husband, twin toddler sons, and a part-time job as a nurse, she wondered, *Why would I want more when my life already feels like it's bursting at the seams? Do you have any idea how much activity two two-year-olds can generate on any given day?*

But because the prayer was short, and because she truly longed for a sense of significance in her life, Dianne began to pray the prayer. Over the next few weeks, God blessed her in many ways, including a promotion at work that would give her more time off and an invitation to teach a ladies Sunday school class at her church—

something she'd wanted to do for a long time.

"Now I realize that God truly does want me to ask in faith for His generous blessings," says Dianne. "And when He sends me new opportunities, because His hand is on me, they don't make my life harder but more meaningful!"

About a year ago, I experienced the kind of meaningful answer to prayer that Dianne describes. During a family vacation, I asked each family member to pray that the Lord would enable me to encourage more women. I thoroughly enjoyed my current opportunities for ministry, which included leading our ministry prayer team and mentoring several young women on a regular basis. But lately I'd been feeling an increased urgency when I prayed, *Expand my territory, Lord!*

God answered every prayer beyond what I could have imagined.

At the time, I imagined that God might increase the number of ladies attending our monthly prayer meeting, or maybe I'd be invited to speak at a women's church retreat.

Instead, less than two months later I was invited to teach an all-day conference to women in South Africa!

I had never taught an all-day conference. I had never even written a workbook for my talks, and I certainly had never been to Africa. Were my borders being stretched? Yes.

Was I out of my comfort zone and did I need the hand of the Lord on me? Definitely!

And guess what God did? He answered every prayer beyond what I could have imagined. As I stood in that South African church before a thousand beautiful women, I was in such awe of the God who responded to my Jabez prayer.

God's plan for you may not include a trip overseas, but what you can know with certainty is that He will give you everything you need to do anything He asks. And He will help you spread wide the apron of your life to take in and hold all the blessings He wants to pour out on you.

Maybe like Dianne you've already read *The Prayer of Jabez* and experienced some amazing miracles of your own, but now you have questions about how to maintain such an exciting life. Perhaps you've seen God at work in powerful ways, but you still long for a deeper understanding of what it means to experience God's hand upon you.

Or maybe this is your first encounter with the prayer of Jabez. Either way, you've come to the right place. Whether you are a businesswoman, a stay-at-home mom, a retiree, or a college student, God is waiting for you to call out to Him like Jabez did. Are you ready to say to God, "I want to see more!"?

God can't wait to lift you into His arms and show you the more that you were made for.

CHAPTER TWO

Invited to Ask

OH, THAT YOU WOULD
BLESS ME INDEED.

ruce and I could hardly contain our joy. Our son was finally here, and now the big question—what to name him? Should it be James Franklin after both our fathers? Or a strong biblical name like Caleb? I remember thinking, *I want this little boy to grow up to be just like his daddy, who seeks after God like…King David.* That was it! The choice was David Bruce.

Choosing just the right name for a child is important to every mother. After all, our prayer is that he or she will live up to it for the rest of his or her life. I believe that Jabez's mother had the same concern for her son. However, in Bible times mothers often chose names that related to their baby's appearance or to the circumstance of the baby's birth. Perhaps that explains why when the big day arrived, "His mother called his name Jabez, saying, 'Because I bore him in pain.'"

We can only guess what excruciating circumstance would have caused this mother to forever wrap her baby in the Hebrew word for pain, *Jabez*. Perhaps she experienced an especially difficult pregnancy or a painful delivery. (When our daughter Jennifer gave birth to our ten-pound, four-ounce grandson, she could have named him Auuuggghhh.) Perhaps the baby was a breech birth, or the labor continued for days before her baby made his entrance into the world. Remember, there were no epidurals or pain relievers to alleviate the pain of childbirth.

Imagine what it must have been like for Jabez to go through childhood with such a name.

Whatever his mother's reason, imagine what it must have been like for Jabez to go through childhood with such a name. Not only did it invite teasing from his friends, but it also cast a shadow over his future. You see, in Bible times a man's name was viewed as a prophecy about his prospects in life. Jabez, it appeared, was destined to cause others pain and to experience much pain himself.

You may be thinking, *My mother should have called me Phooey because she wanted a son. Or maybe the name Mistake because she was sorry she had me—or at least I felt that way growing up.* Perhaps in your past you've been given negative names or you've used negative words to describe yourself, such as *useless, rejected,* or *abused.*

Whatever the circumstances of your life up until now, your past doesn't have to be a picture of your future! I think Jabez understood this. That's why despite his unfortunate beginning Jabez chose to believe something about God that changed his story forever. He believed that God's nature was to bless and that God not only could but also *wanted* to reach down to bless him—and bless him a lot!

Your past doesn't have to be a picture of your future!

How did Jabez get such a big picture of God? Perhaps his mother had told him as a little child about the God of Israel who performed miracle after miracle for his forefathers. Maybe he'd been challenged by the story of Jacob wrestling all night with the angel and saying, "I won't let you go until you bless me!" All we know is that Jabez prayed, "Oh, that You would bless me indeed!"

In the Hebrew language, when the word *indeed* was used, it was like adding five exclamation points or writing it in capital letters and underlining it. Jabez wasn't half asleep, feeling sorry for himself, or mumbling a halfhearted prayer. He was deliberately begging God to bless him and give him a "better view" of what He had in mind for his life.

And that's exactly what happened. God lifted Jabez up out of the ordinary and "granted him what he requested" (1 Chronicles 4:10, NKJV).

THE GOD WHO BLESSES

Do you think about God the way Jabez did—ready and willing to pour out His blessings on those who cry out to Him?

God lifted Jabez up out of the ordinary and "granted him what he requested."

1 CHRONICLES 4:10, NKJV

Tricia didn't have that view of God at all. When this college student from New York first tried to pray the prayer of Jabez, she had a difficult time asking God to bless her. "I could barely get the words out," she admits. "Then I finally realized that part of the problem had to do with my father. He was severely alcoholic and became angry whenever I asked for anything—even his signature on my report card!"

One day, aware of her struggle, the wife of Tricia's pastor challenged her to go to the Bible and read verses that described God's character. What a revolutionary assignment! Tricia was stunned by the many passages revealing God's goodness and His desire to give to His children. She was particularly moved by the words God used when describing Himself to Moses in Exodus 34:6: "merciful and gracious, longsuffering, and abounding in goodness and truth."

Tricia responds and prays to God differently now because she believes that her heavenly Father's arms are open wide, inviting her to ask.

Maybe without meaning to you've pictured God as withholding, not really inclined to bless you. Listen to Psalm 34:10: "Those who seek the LORD shall not lack any good thing." Or perhaps you grew up believing that God is strict and harsh, unwilling to bless you because of your mistakes. Listen to the words of David in Psalm 86:5: "For You, Lord, are good, and ready to forgive, and abundant in mercy to all those who call upon You."

For You, Lord, are good, and ready to forgive, and abundant in mercy to all those who call upon You.

PSALM 86:5

Jesus promised: "Ask, and it will be given to you; seek, and you will find; knock, and it will be opened to you. For *everyone* [including Jabez, you, and me] who asks receives, and he who seeks finds, and to him who knocks it will be opened" (Matthew 7:7–8, emphasis mine).

Jabez didn't have the advantage we have today of reading the words of Jesus and the New Testament writers. Yet long before James wrote the words "every good gift and every perfect gift is from above" (James 1:17), Jabez seemed to know this truth. God longs for you, too, to believe with all your heart that His nature is to give good things to His children. Then you will be able to ask for God's blessings, fully believing that He is delighted by your request.

THE SHAPE OF GOD'S BLESSINGS

At this point, you may agree that God is more generous and giving than you can fathom. But you may also be wondering, *What exactly will it look like in my life when God answers the prayer "Bless me"?*

Who knows better what to give us than God?

The word *bless* in the biblical sense means to impart supernatural favor. When I ask God to bless me, I am crying out for His goodness and favor to be poured out on me. I am also acknowledging that He is the only One who is "able to do exceedingly abundantly above all that we ask or think" (Ephesians 3:20).

Notice that the Bible doesn't record *how* God blessed Jabez, just that He granted his request. If we knew the specifics of Jabez's blessing, we might miss the blessing God wants for us personally and individually because we're looking for something else.

Notice also that Jabez left it entirely up to God to decide what shape—how, when, and in what form—His blessing would come. Who knows better what to give us than God?

Bonnie, who is single, had no doubt that God was blessing her when a friend offered to stack her pile of firewood. But Anita, a grandmother in a nursing home, counted it God's blessing when she received a visit from a relative—something Bonnie might not even think of as a blessing!

This doesn't mean we can't or shouldn't pray for specifics. It just means that praying for a specific need to be met is different than praying "Bless me" and waiting for God to give us what He alone knows will do just that.

Here are some things we do know about the nature of God's blessings.

God's blessing can be either internal or external.

In the previous chapter we read about Dianne, who was blessed with an unexpected promotion at work. That was a tangible blessing from God—something that could be seen and experienced externally, on the physical level. But just as often, God's blessing is something that is meaningful to us personally and is experienced internally, on a spiritual or emotional level.

That was the case with my friend Angie. She'd been in the midst of a family crisis and was feeling, in her own words, "discouraged and unloved." One morning while in prayer she simply asked God to bless her. Around noon she walked to her mailbox and discovered a card from someone she hadn't heard from in months. The letter ended with, "Angie, I just felt like God wanted me to write and say, 'He really loves you and is always there for you.'"

Angie's blessing came in the shape of a letter of encouragement, which represented a personal love note from God. Your blessing might come in the form of an unexpected date with your husband, a timely visit from a relative, a restored relationship, or simply coming across a Scripture verse that speaks specifically to your point of need in that moment.

God's blessing can take place in the midst of difficulty.

When Joan, a full-time wife and mother, began to pray the Jabez prayer, she waited in hopeful anticipation for God's abundant blessing. But instead, everything appeared to get worse. "My husband and I were suddenly fighting more than ever, and our financial situation forced us to go for credit counseling." *Where is God's blessing in all this turmoil?* Joan wondered.

Maybe like Joan your definition of *blessing* automatically assumes money in the bank and a trouble-free life. But Jesus forewarned us, "In the world you will have tribulation"

(John 16:33). And Peter told us, "Do not think it strange concerning the fiery trial which is to try you, as though some strange thing happened to you" (1 Peter 4:12).

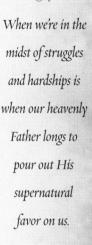

Sometimes the trials we face are simply the natural result of living in a sin-wracked world. They may even come to us as a direct result of the sinful choices of others. However, it is in the midst of these struggles and hardships that our heavenly Father longs to pour out His supernatural favor on all who are willing to ask.

When we're in the midst of struggles and hardships is when our heavenly Father longs to pour out His supernatural favor on us.

Listen to Joan explain how it works: "As I continued to ask God to bless me, He revealed some painful issues my husband and I needed to resolve in order to improve our marriage. God used our conflicts to move us toward a better marriage. And being forced to get credit counseling? It was finally a way out from under our huge mountain of debt. It became obvious to us that my prayer truly was being answered."

God's blessing is not selfish.

God places within each of us as women the natural ability and inclination to nurture others and to make sacrifices for our family. It's gratifying to put ourselves last, or to do without so our loved ones have what they need. Maybe in our effort to be good mothers, we've even admonished our children not to ask for things for themselves. That's usually because we believe or know that asking for something for ourselves means that someone else goes without.

God never has to take away from someone in order to give to someone else.

But that isn't how it works with God! His resources are not limited. He gives His blessings when they're asked for, not on a first come first serve basis. He never has to take away from someone in order to give to someone else. Therefore, He does not view our request for blessing as selfish.

Here's another reason why asking God to bless us is not selfish. The more blessed we become, the more our blessings overflow to others. As you're about to discover in the next chapter, one of God's main purposes in blessing you is so you can then touch others in ways that move them closer to Him.

AN INVITATION TO ASK

Inside the cover of my Bible, I have recorded a little story. It's about a man who once asked Napoleon for an incredible favor. The man knew that he deserved nothing from this great general, yet Napoleon immediately granted his request. When someone inquired as to the reason, Napoleon replied, "He honored me by the magnitude of his request."

God is also honored when you and I come boldly to ask for His blessing and favor. That's because we ask according to His greatness and not according to our worthiness. The kind of blessing we are asking for is not given on the basis of performance but on God's goodness alone. For that reason, God is honored in direct proportion to the magnitude of our request.

The kind of blessing we are asking for is given based on God's goodness alone.

No matter what your circumstances today, God wants to step into your life, like He did with Jabez, and rewrite the rest of your story to include His generous, loving favor. You don't have to change your name. You don't have to change your past. All you have to do is ask, "O God, please bless me, and bless me a lot!"

CHAPTER THREE

A Life without Limits

magine for a moment that you have traveled back in time to spend a day at the home of Jabez. After getting acquainted, Jabez asks you to join him for his morning prayers. You're happy to do so. Together you kneel on the hardened dirt floor of his house. Moments later, you overhear Jabez pleading with God for more blessing, expanded territory, and greater protection. Out of respect, you remain quiet after his "amen."

But later, over a lunch of flatbread and roasted lamb and onions, you just have to ask Jabez a question: "What exactly were you asking God to do for you when you asked Him to expand your territory?"

"Come," Jabez replies, "let me show you." He takes you outside and waves his hand at the acres of land that surround his modest home. "This," he says, "is my territory. It's where my family lives, and it is where I work. It's the place I am responsible to tend. See those sheep and goats?" He points to a grassy area. "I am a farmer and herdsman. I cannot plant more seed or increase my herd unless I have more land. Therefore, every day I cry out to the God of Israel to increase the size of my territory."

You see, when Jabez asked God for a larger territory, he was asking for more than just acres of dirt and more goats. He wanted more business, more responsibility—to multiply that which God had already given him.

Jabez wanted more business, more responsibility—to multiply that which God had already given him.

Whether or not we own land, God has given each of us a territory like Jabez's— a realm of influence for which we're responsible. Your territory begins with the place where you live and work. Your primary dwelling may be a two-bedroom apartment, a house in the country, an office cubicle, a dormitory room, or even a nursing home. Your territory also includes the people you are in a position to impact: your family members, friends, coworkers, neighbors, and even strangers who cross your path. And finally, your territory includes your possessions—not only material belongings, but also your unique gifts and talents.

Try this experiment. Draw a box and then write inside

it words that represent the key people, places, and possessions in your life. Your list might include entries such as "my kids, Andrew and Jonathan" (people); "my part-time job at the hospital" (places); and "my talent for singing" (possessions).

After you've filled up your box, ask yourself how you feel about the size and scope of your territory. Are you satisfied? I hope you're not! Strange as that sounds, I believe that God wants you to hunger for and ask for more.

God wants you to hunger for and ask for more.

But more of what? When we pray, "Enlarge my territory," we're not asking for more acreage to grow crops or feed animals (that is, unless we're farmers). We're asking for more of what we have been given. The word in the Bible used for *territory* could also be translated "coast" or "borders." When we plead with God to expand our borders, we're asking Him to remove the limits on what we can do and who we can become. We're begging Him to throw wide open the doors of opportunity and enlarge our place in this world.

GOD'S EXPANSION PROGRAM

I remember the first time I heard a teaching on this part of the Jabez prayer. My immediate response was, "More?

Whoa…wait a minute. Let me check my Day-Timer." At that point I was a full-time wife and mother—so busy with two toddlers in diapers that I didn't even have time to keep a Day-Timer. Why would I ask God to give me more?

The answer didn't become obvious to me until I placed two words directly behind the word *more*. They were the words *for You*. Eventually I realized that by asking God for more territory, I was really saying to God, "Let me do more for You. Expand my territory so that I can have a greater impact for You."

> *"God, let me do more for You.*
>
> *Expand my territory so that I can have a greater impact for You."*

Can you imagine your child coming to you one day and saying, "Mom, may I have more responsibility? I want to do more for you"? How would you respond (after he or she helped you up off the floor)? Imagine how God feels when you, His child, come to Him expressing your desire to be given more so that you might use it to influence others for Him.

Because your request brings God joy, you can be certain that He will answer you when you ask in faith for more territory. But what will His answers look like, particularly for us women?

Let's consider three ways God may choose to answer our cry for more.

God will expand your territory right where you stand.

When Jesus told the disciples to be witnesses for Him, He told them to start right at home—Jerusalem—in their own backyard. As wives, mothers, daughters, widows, or single women, the most important territory we are given is our loved ones and our closest friends. God doesn't ask us to neglect our home turf to go looking for greener pastures someplace else. Instead, He helps us discover the amazing potential we have to impact the world right from our own living room.

Perhaps you are like Dottie, who is single and living in an apartment. Her territory is expanding through a particular talent and hobby. Dottie loves to quilt, and she has several teenage girls from her church over to her apartment for breakfast every Saturday morning. "We eat, laugh, talk, and pray together," she says. "And then I teach them how to quilt." What a great way to do what she enjoys as she disciples these young girls for the Lord.

Maybe like Martha you have grandchildren who live in another state or are already grown. Once a month, Martha invites the children of a single mom to her home to bake cookies. The mom enjoys the free time and the kids have fun. They even get to take their yummy creations home for dessert.

Part of God's plan for expanding your territory could include your raising children who will someday accomplish great things for God's kingdom. Like Billy Graham's mother, you may raise a son who is destined to touch the lives of millions.

God may also expand your territory through your husband. Your support and encouragement can make a tremendous difference in his ability to accomplish what God has called him to do.

The wife described in Proverbs 31 exemplifies this principle. She was a woman of great influence and used her talents to serve people near and far, yet her husband and her family remained her first priority. We're told in verses 12 and 27, "She does [her husband] good…. She looks well to the ways of her household" (NASB). We also learn that she speaks kindly to her children, rises early to care for them, and makes sure all her family's needs for food and clothing are met. As a result, "The heart of her husband safely trusts her; so he will have no lack of gain…. Her children rise up and call her blessed" (vv. 11, 28).

God will expand your territory by asking you to step up.

Sometimes God will ask you to step up to a new opportunity in order to expand your territory beyond where you stand.

Remember Dianne, mother of twins from chapter 1, who said that God blessed her by giving her a women's Bible class at her church? After several years, Dianne's strong gift for teaching became apparent to those in leadership, and they asked her to become the women's ministry teacher. This enabled her to impact every woman in her church. Dianne "stepped up" to a bigger arena, and now her territory extends from her home into her church community.

Sueann, a young mother with three small children, saw her territory extend across the street in her neighborhood.

Sueann, a young mother with three small children, saw her territory extend across the street. When her neighbor Jeannie's husband left her, Jeannie needed to work a part-time job to provide for their two children. "Taking care of Jeannie's little boys three days a week," Sueann says, "has opened up many opportunities for me to show God's love to them and their mother." As a result of her efforts, several other women in the neighborhood have stepped in to offer support and encouragement as well.

God may ask you to step up in a very different way. It may include a new position at work that enables you to start a support group for single moms during lunch hour, volunteering at a crisis pregnancy center to encourage young women, or even going on a church mission trip to help build houses for the homeless.

God wants you to step up to new opportunities to use the lessons you have learned and the talents He has given you.

The Proverbs 31 woman expanded her territory through a variety of avenues. We're told, "She considers a field and buys it; from her earnings she plants a vineyard" (v. 16, NASB). And, "She extends her hand to the poor, and she stretches out her hands to the needy" (v. 20, NASB).

Regardless of who you are or what season of life you're in, God wants you to step up to new opportunities to use the lessons you have learned and the talents He has given you. Jesus always encouraged those whom He had touched to go and tell "what great things the Lord has done for you" (Mark 5:19).

God will expand your territory by asking you to step into someone's life.

Now and then, God will orchestrate divine encounters with people you may or may not know. He'll ask you to step into someone's life momentarily to minister to or help that person in some way. You might call these Jabez Appointments. They could take place with a passenger you sit next to on a flight, the woman waiting next to you in the doctor's office, or the repairman who shows up to fix your washing machine.

A friend of mine named Pat told me that her car recently broke down on a very secluded road. After several attempts to restart the car, she prayed, *Father, please start my car so I can make it to a service station.* The engine started on the next try, and she drove to the nearest repair shop. Looking under the hood, the mechanic asked, "How did you get here?"

Apparently, a cable was missing from the engine that should have made it impossible for the car to run. Pat, recognizing this as a Jabez Appointment, told the man that God had gotten her there in answer to her prayer. This led very naturally into a conversation about how much God is concerned with every aspect of our lives.

> *God allows people to step into our territory so we can plant seeds that He can then water and cause to grow.*

One woman I know loves to stand in the longest checkout line at the grocery store in order to speak to the woman in front of or behind her. "I compliment her on her new baby or the color of her blouse," she says. "I look for a way to encourage her and let her know she's special."

You see, God allows people to step into our territory— or us into theirs—so we can plant seeds that He can then water and cause to grow. Our job is simply to be on the lookout for these amazing encounters.

BRING WHAT YOU HAVE

If you're like most women today, chances are you already feel pulled in too many directions. You're tired, overworked, and overstressed. Even though you long to impact more people for God, you wonder where you'll find the time or energy.

I understand! That's why it's so important to grasp the fact that asking for expanded territory isn't just asking God for more to do. Rather, it is a whole new way of looking at your life and the opportunities that come your way.

You may be thinking, *I'm not certain that I have anything to offer or that God wants to use what I have.* Then let me share an insight with you from the last chapter of the Gospel of John. As you may recall, the disciples had fished all night and caught nothing. Jesus is standing on the shore, and He tells them to cast their net on the right side of the boat. The Bible says that they are not able to draw the net in because of the multitude of fish.

As they approach the shore, they see a bed of burning coals and fish already being prepared for their hungry stomachs. Yet listen to what Jesus says next: "Bring some of the fish which you have just caught." What? They had just seen Jesus feed thousands with a handful of fish. He did not need them to contribute anything to the fish that were roasting on the fire.

But Jesus says, "Bring what *you* have." He knew how much those hungry men loved the taste of their own fresh fish—even though He was responsible for what they caught that morning. He also knows that when you and I bring what we have been given, He can use it to feed the hungry souls all around us as well. It doesn't matter what you have. What matters is that you bring it and place it in His hands to use in whatever way He desires.

Expanding our territory leaves us exhilarated, not exhausted.

The process looks something like this:

- Ask God to let me do more for Him;
- Aim to be available to those around me;
- Approach surprise encounters as potential Jabez Appointments;
- Acknowledge it's about God's agenda, not mine.

When we take this approach, we discover that expanding our territory leaves us exhilarated, not exhausted.

This doesn't mean we'll never be required to sacrifice, to work hard at something, or to fit a new activity into our schedule. It does mean that because God wants only our best, we can trust Him to help us arrange our lives in a way that energizes rather than saps us. God knows how He has gifted you and what your time schedule looks like. In fact, His plan for your "more" may actually mean you do *less* of something good simply because it's not where you're most productive or because it drains you.

Are you a wife and mother with a blended family to care for? Maybe God wants to use you to bring healing and hope to hurting families. Perhaps you're a single woman whose job requires you to be on the road a lot. Could it be that God wants to use you to encourage a fellow passenger or lonely coworker? Or maybe you're a single mom trying to work outside the home, teach an aerobics class, and raise three teenagers. Maybe God will bring more opportunities to care for the friends your teens bring home.

All of this means you will need to use discernment as your territory expands. Not every invitation is one you should accept, and not every stranger is one you should approach. Pray for wisdom and ask the Holy Spirit to guide you. Be sure that your motives are right—God's glory, not yours. Strive to keep your priorities straight—loved ones come before careers or even church functions. And always keep in mind that God wants to expand your territory in ways that not only bring Him honor, but also bring you delight.

A widow recently sent us her story explaining that she'd always been a behind-the-scenes person, so she worried what God might ask her to do when she prayed, *Let me do more for You*. One day her associate pastor called and asked if she would be willing to have the church staff over to her home for breakfast the following Saturday morning. Not only did she love to cook, but that request was also the answer to her prayer. "When I opened the door that Saturday morning," she said, "I was smiling from ear to ear. None of them will ever know how much that meant to me."

AN ETERNAL HARVEST

It is such a rewarding experience to see God personally say yes to this particular part of the prayer. Not just because we get to see our territory expanded, but because we get to see *God's* territory expanded through ours.

Think about it. We all know people who have large territories, in the sense that they have a great amount of influence, wealth, and maybe even property. But what God cares about is what that territory produces. Is it an earthly or an eternal harvest? Is it a land producing fruit for God or is it going to waste?

Having more influence and responsibility is great. But only when we use our territory to minister, or to reach others for Christ, does it glorify God. As we continue to reach outward with our influence, He reaches into hearts and changes lives. No wonder God loves to answer this part of the prayer!

Only when we use our territory to minister, or to reach others for Christ, does it glorify God.

Today I urge you to ask God not only to expand your territory, but also to bless it greatly and use it for His purposes. Picture your entire territory in your mind right now—all the people, places, and possessions in your life. Thank God for all He has given you. Then tell Him you want Him to multiply it over and over. Ask Him to expand your territory beyond your wildest dreams, until it reaches as far and wide as He would have it, even to the ends of the earth!

CHAPTER FOUR

When God Steps In

OH, THAT YOUR HAND
WOULD BE WITH ME!

he children were getting restless, but our Sunday morning service was about to end…or so I thought. At the conclusion of his message, our pastor shared a heartbreaking story. A teenager from another state had become pregnant. "She has been abandoned by her parents," he explained, "and she needs a place to live for the next six months." Immediately I sensed that God was about to expand my territory. It was as if the Lord gently whispered, "Darlene, this invitation is for you."

But, *Lord*, I reasoned, *our children are so young. I know nothing about dealing with teenagers. And how will my husband feel about this?*

During the drive home, I discovered that God had spoken to Bruce's heart in a similar way. So we said, "Yes,

> *It was as if the Lord gently whispered, "Darlene, this invitation is for you."*

Lord, we will take this girl into our home
for You." With the decision confirmed, we
made the arrangements. Jody would arrive
the following day.

Convinced that
you're unequal to
the task, you're
overcome by fear,
inadequacy, and
apprehension.

That afternoon I became overwhelmed
with feelings of fear and inadequacy. What
had I been thinking? Retreating to the back
porch with my Bible, I poured out my
trembling heart to the Lord. *Father, I*
pleaded, I can't do this! What if she's on drugs?
How will I know what to say? I feel so weak and
unprepared to handle this girl's problems. Please, please help me!

Maybe you recognize this kind of situation in your own
life. You eagerly say yes to an exciting border-expanding
opportunity—only to realize that you've gotten yourself
in way over your head. Convinced that you're unequal
to the task, you're overcome by fear, inadequacy, and
apprehension. You may even wonder, *Am I in the right place?*

As you are about to discover, the wonderful truth is that
you're right where God wants you!

OUT ON A LIMB

There's a reason why Jabez's third request, "Oh, that Your
hand would be with me," follows his request for more

territory. Up to this point, Jabez probably felt that he could handle the challenges his territory required. After all, how hard is it to feed a few goats and keep up a small plot of land? But if God gave him *more* territory, it would mean more responsibility and greater challenges. Jabez understood that he would not be able to succeed without God's divine help and intervention.

In the same way, you may have felt capable of handling what lay ahead *before* you started asking for more territory. And if a new opportunity came along and you felt uncomfortable—not skilled or talented enough—you found a way to avoid it. You pretended not to notice that woman alone in the restaurant crying, or you told yourself you were just too busy to minister to the women in your neighborhood or office.

In order to expand your borders beyond where they are, God wants to move you beyond where you are.

Those are understandable reactions. But in order to expand your borders beyond where they are, God wants to move you beyond where *you* are—all the way out on a limb, you might say.

Why? Not so He can leave you hanging there or let you fall, but so you will learn to cry out for *His* hand, *His* help, *His* touch on your life. Only then can He do through you what you can't do alone. And only then will He be glorified by your accomplishments—because it's obvious that they couldn't have happened any other way!

What an intimate image the words *keep Your hand on me* paint. The picture is of a loving God placing His hand on you so that His power and presence are there in your moment of need. As you step out of your comfort zone into unfamiliar territory for Him, this is an accurate description of exactly what God wants to do for you!

BY HIS SPIRIT

Throughout the Old Testament, the "hand of God" represented His power, His presence, and His provision for His people. When Jabez prayed for God's hand, he was literally asking God to give him every kind of divine help possible for every challenge or opportunity he faced. But Jabez would have experienced the hand of God in a new and even more dramatic way had he lived during the time of Jesus.

You see, the disciples were also motivated and headed for their expanded territory—Judea, Samaria, and all the world—when Jesus stopped them. "He commanded them not to leave Jerusalem, but to wait for what the Father had promised, 'which,' He said, 'you heard of from Me'" (Acts 1:4, NASB). The disciples must have wondered what power they could possibly need after being trained for three years by Jesus Himself—watching Him work, hearing Him pray. But on the day of Pentecost, God's hand—His power and presence—would come upon them in the person of His Holy Spirit (Acts 1:8). Only then were they empowered to do the miraculous things we read about in the book of Acts.

Today you and I receive God's Holy Spirit at the time of our salvation (Acts 2:38). God wants so desperately to be with us that He chooses to place His own Spirit within us. This happens at the very moment we accept, by faith, His Son's death on the cross as the payment for our sins. Not only does He want to spend eternity with us; He wants to spend today with us. But you and I still have the choice to ignore Him or invite Him to be active in our everyday lives.

Obviously, it's to our advantage to follow the command to "walk in the Spirit" (Galatians 5:16), be "led by the Spirit" (Galatians 5:18), and be "filled with the Spirit" (Ephesians 5:18) on an ongoing basis. When we ask our heavenly Father to place His hand upon us, we are asking that His presence and provision come to us through the power of His Holy Spirit. It is not our power but God's power in and through us that we're seeking.

It comes as no surprise that experiencing God's hand on us is essential as we seek to expand our territory. He gives us discernment, supernatural power, encouragement, and strength to do His will—on the spot as we cry out for it!

But here's something I really don't want you to miss. We shouldn't limit our request for God's hand on us to ministry situations or opportunities to expand our territory. God's hand is just as powerful and just as available to us in other kinds of situations we face every day. When we pray, "Keep Your hand on me," we're not just asking God, "Put Your hand on me for the next hour while I'm speaking." We're asking for God's hand to be with us at all times.

GOD'S HAND IN ACTION

You understand what it means to ask for God's hand and why you need it. But how is the hand of God actually experienced in the lives of different women in their various circumstances? Let's take a look at some snapshots that show how God's hand provides for us in key arenas.

God's hand at work in your ministry opportunities.

Perhaps like Deb you feel a little intimidated about sharing your faith. "I sensed the Lord wanted me to invite my neighbor over for coffee," she says, "and I needed His hand on me to overcome my fear of being rejected."

Once her neighbor was finally seated in Deb's cozy red

kitchen, Deb found herself able to naturally share her testimony, which led into a discussion about spiritual things. "God's hand not only provided the boldness I needed," she says, "but it also gave me the right words to say in answer to her sometimes pointed or difficult questions."

Deb's comments echo those of Luke in the book of Acts concerning the crowd's reaction to Peter and John's preaching. "When they saw the boldness of Peter and John, and perceived that they were uneducated and untrained men, they marveled. And they realized that they had been with Jesus" (4:13). What made the people marvel wasn't their qualifications, but their lack of them!

That's not to say God doesn't use our gifts. As you will recall from the last chapter, Dianne's gift for speaking led to her territory being expanded into her church community, which included speaking at their fall women's retreat. After every session and sometimes into the night, women sought her counsel about their heartbreaking problems. "As I begin to speak with each woman," Dianne says, "I am so aware that only God's hand can provide, through me, what they need to hear. They need His answers, not mine."

Whatever God is encouraging you to do for Him in a ministry setting—whether public or private—you can be sure that His hand will provide just what is needed, when you ask.

God's hand at work in your family.

If you're a parent, you probably already know that there are few areas where we need God's hand more! Brooke knew that God's hand was her only hope in raising her son successfully. Having lost her husband to cancer just six months before, she was heartbroken over rebellious choices her teenager, Jeff, had been making recently. She realized that Jeff was still grief-stricken and angry about his dad's death.

One day after a heated argument, Jeff slammed the door to his bedroom, and Brooke tearfully retreated to her own room and knelt next to her bed. *Father,* she prayed, *please put Your hand on our son. I can't reach him and I can't fix the pain he is feeling. Show me, Lord, how to pray for him.*

God's hand will provide just what is needed, when you ask.

An hour passed. Still on her knees, Brooke heard a knock on the door. "Mom." Jeff's voice was quiet. "Can I come in?" Jeff then told her how, in his frustration, he had opened his Bible for the first time in six months and discovered a letter from his dad. It had been written and placed there the day before he left for the hospital. "Dad told me all the things I would be feeling toward God after he died," he said, "and then he reminded me that God never makes mistakes."

Jeff went on to tell his mom how he had gotten on his knees to ask God's forgiveness and that he now wanted hers as well.

Are you struggling with a rebellious child, a colicky baby, or an obnoxious relative? Ask for God's hand to be on you! He can bring you favor with others and give you wisdom to know how to pray and what to say. He can provide you with just the right

Ask for God's hand to be on you!

insight into a problem. God's hand is powerful to do in our families what we could never accomplish on our own.

God's hand at work in your marriage.

Those of us who are married know that even in the best of circumstances, we need God's hand to enable us to encourage and assist our husbands to be everything God wants them to be. Christine is married to an angry and, at times, insensitive man. "I need God's hand daily," she confesses, "to provide the gentleness that enables me to give the kind of soft answer that turns away wrath [Proverbs 15:1] as I try to minister to and be a good wife to my husband."

Danielle has an invalid husband, so she sees God's hand provide differently. "When I'm exhausted," she reports, "God provides the strength and patience I need to genuinely love doing the things my husband needs me to do for him."

Whatever your marriage challenges, you need only to ask the One whose resources are unlimited.

However, don't limit your thinking to God helping you with only the negatives in life. For example, maybe it's because you prayed for God's hand on you today that it occurred to you to stop and pick up a rosebush for your husband's fledgling garden. Or maybe the presence of His hand is evident in your mood, your spirit, your tone of voice. Think about it. God's Spirit can give you great insight into how you can best pray for your husband in times of difficulty as well as when things are going great. You need God's hand on you on a daily basis simply to know what to say or how to best meet his needs. God can show you ways to help your husband achieve his dreams. Who knows the number of ways your marriage can benefit when you are asking for God's hand!

God's hand at work in the marketplace.

Susan works for a boss who is hard to please and quick to think the worst. One morning Susan was called into the manager's office. Her boss was angry and loudly began making accusations against Susan that weren't true. "My first reaction was to get angry and defensive," she says. "But then I silently prayed that God would help me know what to do."

Very gently and respectfully, Susan responded to her supervisor's derogatory questions. Her kind and confident manner slowly eased the tension in the room.

"When the crisis was over," Susan says, "I knew God's hand had provided the peace I needed to remain calm in the midst of an explosive situation."

Conflicts like Susan's happen every day in the workplace. We experience challenges to our integrity, pressure to put work first. And all too often the demands of coping with a variety of personalities lead to conflicts of some kind. Isn't it wonderful to know that God's hand can be on you in the midst of challenges you face during a busy day at work? Even if you're thinking about a million other things, because you have asked for His power and presence you can experience the wonderful benefits of His nearness, including the "peace of God, which surpasses all understanding" (Philippians 4:7).

Isn't it wonderful to know that God's hand can be on you in the midst of challenges you face during a busy day at work?

BREAKING THROUGH TO DEPENDENCE

At the opening of this chapter, I was out on my porch overwhelmed with doubts about my ability to handle a pregnant teen. Let me tell you what happened next. As I listed all of my weaknesses for God, I noticed something moving on the cement floor next to my foot. I looked closer and discovered the smallest ant I'd ever seen…and it was dragging a huge, dead bee!

I watched its progress with rapt attention and thought, *Incredible! This is like me trying to drag a car down the highway!*

And then I got it. If God can put enough strength into this tiny creature to pull something fifty times its size, He will give me the strength I need to accomplish something for Him that appears too huge to handle.

As I listed all of my weaknesses for God, I noticed something moving on the cement floor next to my foot.

That day was a turning point for me, a breakthrough to dependence. I realized that God is not limited by my weaknesses but liberated by them! Through my weakness God gets to be great and reveal His amazing power. No wonder Jesus told Paul, "My grace is sufficient for you, for My strength is made perfect in weakness" (2 Corinthians 12:9).

Often we are mistaken about how this works, aren't we? When we feel weak, rather than asking God for His strength, we try harder to be strong. We may even ask Him to *make us* strong. But when we do this, we rob God of an opportunity to reveal *His* perfect strength through our weakness. The right response is to say to God, "I can't do this. But I know You can. And then everyone will know it's You, not me, who is strong!"

The next time you find yourself in a situation in which you need God's hand on you, I want you to try something. Write down a list of your shortcomings. Then notice something. You've written "I am… I am…" There's your mistake. God wants your focus on Him, not on you. Have you ever wondered why God refers to Himself as "I AM"? Over the years, when I've been tempted to say, "But God, I am weak…" or "God, I am afraid…" I've found it helpful to imagine God saying the opposite: "I AM your strength, I AM your courage, I AM whatever you need, because 'I AM WHO I AM'" (Exodus 3:14; John 8:58).

You see, God isn't scanning the horizon looking for superwomen. He is actively looking for those who will believe and trust Him to do what is humanly impossible…just like Esther.

That day was a turning point for me, a breakthrough to dependence.

FOR SUCH A TIME

Remember the story? God unexpectedly enlarged Esther's territory by placing her in the king's palace where she became

Queen of Persia. One day her cousin Mordecai informed her of Haman's devious plot to destroy her people, the Jews. She was then asked to intercede on their behalf by going before the king. Her natural reaction was fear and hesitancy. After all, the king could have her killed for such an action.

God isn't scanning the horizon looking for superwomen. He is actively looking for those who will believe and trust Him to do what is humanly impossible.

Then Mordecai sent her a message that included these insightful words: "Who knows whether you have come to the kingdom for such a time as this?" (Esther 4:14). Would she depend upon her own strength and courage or would she look to the One who is all-powerful?

Esther sent word to Mordecai to gather all the Jews of the city to fast for her, neither eating nor drinking for three days and nights. She said, "My maids and I will fast likewise." Only on the third day did she venture into the king's inner court, and the rest of her story is history.

- Esther recognized that she was powerless to save herself or her people.
- Esther remembered that God had placed her where

she was for a reason—His purposes and her destiny.

- Esther realized that she needed God's powerful hand on her regardless of the outcome.

That's the way it works for you and me as well. First we look at our expanded territory and see how weak and helpless we are to accomplish what God has asked us to do. Next, we remember that God has strategically placed us right where we are for this time in history according to His plan. Finally, we recognize that it is God's hand upon us that is powerful. And we don't want to miss the opportunity to experience the greatness of our God.

We don't want to miss the opportunity to experience the greatness of our God.

THE TOUCH OF GREATNESS

Take a moment to think about the areas in your life where you need a touch of God's greatness. You may want to write down in your journal some situations where you know you need God's hand to be with you. Then commit to pray the next time you face that circumstance, relying upon God to come through for you.

Through living with Jody, I discovered that depending on the hand of God is a moment-by-moment process.

Eventually, Jody became like part of our family. But more important, while she was with us she became part of God's family. She was challenged to exercise her new faith almost immediately when she decided to allow a Christian couple to adopt her baby. The choice was agonizing. But how much harder it would have been had Jody not been able to trust in God!

Depending on the hand of God is a moment-by-moment process.

Isn't it wonderful to realize that we are all works in progress? Whether you are a new believer or a mature Christian, God knows exactly where you are in your Christian walk and what you're capable of understanding. Remember, God is more than willing to teach you how to depend upon Him on a regular basis. He will answer your prayer as surely as He answered Esther's and Jabez's. All you have to do is ask, "Oh, that Your hand would be with me!"

CHAPTER FIVE

Safe to Succeed

OH, THAT YOU WOULD
KEEP ME FROM EVIL.

S ue sat at my kitchen table looking confused and discouraged. "This can't be happening," she said, shaking her head. "Cyndee and I have always gotten along so well. God was blessing our friendship and our ministry. What went wrong?"

For years, Sue and her best friend Cyndee had pursued their dream of a career in music together. I had personally seen God's Spirit powerfully at work through them during performances as they sang and shared what God had done in their lives. Recently, they'd completed their first recording—a dream come true.

But now, Sue told me, things had come to a screeching halt. During a recent rehearsal, it became obvious that she and Cyndee were not in agreement about the details of an upcoming event. "We said terrible things to each other," Sue confessed, "and became so angry that we haven't spoken to each other in three weeks."

Can you relate to Sue's experience? God is answering your prayers and blessing you. He is giving you more territory, more to do for Him. You're learning how to walk in the Spirit and are experiencing God's hand on you in ways you had not thought possible. Then suddenly the unexpected takes place—sin enters the picture—and like Sue you wonder, *What happened?*

I believe that Jabez anticipated just such a scenario when he prayed the fourth part of his prayer, "Oh, that You would keep me from evil!" Apparently, Jabez understood something that many of us miss: When God blesses us and expands our territory, we aren't *less* tempted to sin (though it might feel that way); we are more likely to be tempted!

Then suddenly the unexpected takes place—sin enters the picture.

You see, those who are content to do a few things for God don't bother Satan. Those who remain in their comfort zone pose little or no threat to him. But when you begin to take territory for God, guess whose territory you're invading?

Once you genuinely commit to let God do amazing things through you and then depend on His supernatural power to accomplish His agenda, Satan takes notice. He knows we cannot continue to live the abundant life, enjoy God's blessing, and do more for our Lord if evil and sin prevail in our lives. That's why the Bible tells us that "your adversary the devil walks about like a roaring lion, seeking whom he may devour" (1 Peter 5:8).

Are you beginning to see why this part of Jabez's prayer is so vital?

Let's take a closer look at exactly what Jabez was asking God to do for him.

KEEP AWAY

The first thing I want you to notice about Jabez's final request is what he *didn't* say. Jabez did not ask God to keep him or protect him in the *midst* of the evil. He didn't pray, "Keep me *through* evil," or "Help me to overcome it." No! He prayed, "Keep me *from* evil." Don't even let me approach that which will tempt me to sin.

When you begin to take territory for God, guess whose territory you're invading?

All too often this strategy is the exact opposite of how you and I attempt to remain strong for God. We take a look at the wonderfully amazing things God is doing in and through us, and we mistakenly conclude, "I can handle this temptation," rather than "I need God to keep temptation far from me."

The difference between these two approaches is critical. That's because sin is always preceded by temptation. Therefore, if we can *avoid* temptation, if we can keep from even encountering it, we are less likely to sin. This coincides with what Jesus taught us. Jesus told His disciples to "pray that you may not enter into temptation" (Luke 22:40). And when they asked Him how to pray, Jesus gave them the Lord's Prayer, which includes the request "do not lead us into temptation" (Matthew 6:13).

So then the prayer "Keep me from evil" is a request for God Himself to keep temptation from even knocking on our door.

My friend Jessica has experienced how this works. "One night my husband and I had a heated argument right before he left on a business trip," she says. "Knowing how vulnerable he would be, I pleaded with God to keep evil away from him. I knew that God could divert the advances of an attractive woman in the hotel lobby who might have her eye on him. Or shield him from actions or thoughts that would tempt him to watch inappropriate cable stations. It was encouraging to realize that John could be saved from a fight he might be too weak to take on—and not even know it!"

When was the last time you asked God to keep evil away from you or away from your husband…your child… your friend…or your pastor?

Praying this part of the Jabez prayer does not eliminate all our temptations. It's not a magic shield protecting us or those we love. Likewise, it doesn't mean we get to just sit back and count on God to do everything to keep evil or Satan at bay. As you're about to discover, we have a crucial part to play as well. You and I must make sure that while we're asking God to keep temptation far from us we're not inviting it to come near by making wrong choices.

OUR PART IN "KEEP AWAY"

When it comes to avoiding temptation, often we're our own worst enemy. We're like Samson when he revealed to Delilah exactly what would make him weak, leaving himself wide open to attack. (You can read this story in Judges 16.)

When it comes to avoiding temptation, often we're our own worst enemy.

One of Satan's main tactics is to tempt us where we're weakest. Our part in "keep away," then, is to acknowledge those areas where we're vulnerable and take proactive, preventive measures to avoid being tempted.

A friend told me a humorous story that illustrates what I mean. A woman who was dieting asked God to keep her away from all desserts. One evening she began to head for the refrigerator, where her son's leftover birthday cake was stored. Immediately, the telephone rang. Her second attempt was interrupted by someone knocking at her door. She suddenly realized that God was answering her prayer and keeping her from going to the refrigerator where she would be tempted to indulge.

She humbly thanked God for doing His part. Then she did hers. She saved one piece of cake for her son and gave the rest to a neighbor.

Are you beginning to see it? When we genuinely cry out to God to keep temptation away from us, He will act on our behalf. He is powerful to keep and to save us! But then *we* need to do everything in our power to avoid the temptation. We can cancel a questionable subscription, or we can avoid a store where we have a proven history of overspending. We can pray before we meet with that person who tends to rub us the wrong way. Or we can ask a close friend to hold us accountable in an area where we're prone to sin.

We need to do everything in our power to avoid temptation.

All of these are ways we can do our part when we ask God to keep us from evil.

THE TEMPTATIONS OF WOMEN

It seems relatively easy to come up with categories of temptations that men struggle with, particularly sexual sin. But what kinds of unique temptations do women most often struggle with?

So far we've mentioned pride and overeating among the temptations we face (as do men!). But since knowing where we're weak is so critical, it makes sense to consider what temptations women tend to encounter on a regular basis.

I recently asked a group of women that question. Here are some of their responses:

- tempted to complain when things don't go my way
- tempted to compare myself to others
- tempted to compromise what I know is right
- tempted not to tell the whole truth
- tempted to hold a grudge and refuse to forgive
- tempted to be critical of others
- tempted to be jealous of others
- tempted to gossip
- tempted to be discontent with what I have
- tempted to waste time, such as spending too much time watching television
- tempted to fantasize about being married to another man

- tempted to indulge in books or media with questionable content
- tempted to get angry and lose control
- tempted to yell or lash out at my kids

Are you nodding your head at any of these? Some of these temptations are obvious choices for the "keep away" approach we just discussed. Don't buy the fudge and you won't be tempted to eat it. Don't buy inappropriate novels—instead stock up on good alternatives.

But notice that many of these temptations are the kind that sneak up on us unawares. That's partly because they have to do with invisible, intangible things that we don't always see coming, such as feelings, attitudes, and relationship issues.

This shouldn't surprise us since as women we're wired to be both emotional and relational. Think about it. If you ask a man to list his temptations, many of them begin outside him. If you ask a woman to list temptations, she'll probably start talking about feelings—anger, resentment, jealousy. And she'll probably mention relationship dynamics—respecting her boss or submitting to her husband, for example.

Understanding better the nature of our temptations helps us take steps to avoid them. For example, we may need to take certain precautions when we're tired or emotionally fragile. Or we may realize that we need to do some work in a relationship in order to avoid a recurring temptation to sin in anger.

I'd like to gently challenge you today to ask the Lord, "What are the three areas in which I experience the most temptation to sin?" Then record the answers in your journal. Notice how many of your answers have to do with your attitude, your thought life, or your responses to others. Ask God to keep you from these temptations. Ask Him to show you how you can better keep *yourself* away. Then follow James's advice: "Therefore submit to God. Resist the devil and *he* will flee from *you*" (James 4:7, emphasis mine).

Understanding better the nature of our temptations helps us take steps to avoid them.

WINNING MOVES

Up until now we've been talking about how we can take detours to avoid temptation altogether. But what happens when you miss the off-ramp and slam straight into temptation?

When you find yourself in this position (and you will), the most important thing to remember is that God has given us two very powerful promises. First, He guarantees that you *can* walk away from the temptation you face, if you choose to. God promises in 1 Corinthians 10:13 that He "will not allow you to be tempted beyond what you are able." That's amazing, isn't it?

Second, God tells us that He will personally make a way of escape for us. He'll provide a means for us to bear the temptation or to get loose from its clutches altogether. (Remember the woman who couldn't make it to her refrigerator for that cake?)

These two promises are like God's strong arms around us when we find ourselves face-to-face with temptation. They give us confidence that no temptation *has* to lead to sin. Now let me share with you three very practical ways that you can do your part to stand on these promises and defeat temptation.

Believe the truth—not the lie.

Satan is a deceiver. He attempts to rob us of God's truth, and in its place he proposes subtle, deceptive untruths, such as *I couldn't help myself…I'll never be able to…I can't believe that God will…*

Because we know that God's truth sets us free and keeps us free (John 8:32), we can be victorious over temptation by letting Scripture restore God's truth to our mind. Remember how Jesus responded when Satan tempted Him? He stated out loud what was true, and Satan couldn't argue.

Jenn, a professional woman from Miami, found herself faced with the temptation to let fear rule her. "I was learning a new procedure at work," she explains. "And I became paralyzed by all sorts of fearful thoughts like, *What if I can't do this and I lose my job? Why am I so dumb?*"

Then Jenn remembered 2 Timothy 1:7, which says, "God has not given us a spirit of fear." Immediately she went into the ladies restroom, closed the door, and prayed out loud, "Lord, since this spirit of fear is not from You, I refuse to believe the lie that I can't do this. Instead, I choose to believe the truth

We can be victorious over temptation by letting Scripture restore God's truth to our mind.

that 'I can do all things through Christ who strengthens me.' I will learn this procedure and give You the glory."

A sense of peace and calm replaced her inner turmoil, and she returned to her desk unhindered by fearful thoughts. She attacked the lie by stating the truth.

Take your thoughts captive.

If you have teenagers, you know that at times it's tempting to let negative or critical thoughts take over. Rachel had become increasingly frustrated with her son's lack of responsibility in taking care of his dog, his clothes, his CD collection, and even his baseball gear. "Every time I saw an empty dog dish or yet another T-shirt on the bathroom floor," she says, "I would start thinking, *Mitch is so irresponsible…I can't depend on him for anything. Why can't he be more like his sister?*"

By the time Mitch got home from school, Rachel's negative thinking had made her so upset that she exploded. "My relationship with Mitch was disintegrating, until I heard a discussion on Christian radio one morning. It was about bringing every thought into captivity to the obedience of Christ (see 2 Corinthians 10:5).

"As I took charge of my negative thoughts and brought them before the Lord," Rachel said, "I realized that Mitch needed my instruction, not my criticism. Rather than overreact with anger, Rachel mentally locked up her negative thoughts and refused to reopen that box. She was then able to calmly carry out consequences that encouraged Mitch to take his responsibilities seriously.

Choose to be humble.

When you are tempted to complain, be critical, become angry, or refuse to forgive, ask yourself this question. What character quality is missing when you neglect to "let this mind be in you which was also in Christ Jesus" (Philippians 2:5)? The answer is usually "humility."

In Sue and Cyndee's situation, pride was the evil that hindered their relationship and temporarily halted their ministry. Fortunately, Sue and Cyndee realized that they'd both allowed their need to be "right," or get their own way, interfere with what God wanted to do through them. They humbled themselves and forgave each other. Then they committed to pray together for humility and grace before each rehearsal.

Throwing humility in front of temptation is like throwing a bucket of water on a fire.

Throwing humility in front of temptation is like throwing a bucket of water on a fire. Temptations simply cannot conceive and then bear sin in an environment of humility!

Karen and her mother had not been on friendly terms for years. Since Karen had become a Christian, she noticed her mother's lack of love even more. One morning, as Karen read Matthew 18, the Lord spoke to her about the parable on forgiveness. She reasoned that her mother should be the one to ask forgiveness. But God continued to gently remind Karen of what He wanted her to do.

"I cried for days," she says, "before I was able to truly

humble myself and not insist on having my own way." Karen went to her mother and genuinely asked her forgiveness for the things she knew had hurt their relationship. "My mom may never ask my forgiveness, but our communication has improved dramatically because I was willing, with God's help, to say, 'I'm sorry for hurting you.'"

It's not easy to take your thoughts captive, humble yourself, or renew your mind. But God promises to give us His grace and strength as we entrust ourselves into His loving hands. Only then can we discover that His ways are so far above our ways. And choosing to do things God's way will keep us from something else that Jabez knew all about....

THAT I MIGHT NOT CAUSE PAIN

Jabez had a reason quite apart from his honorable character for asking God to keep him from evil. He included it right in his prayer—"that I may not cause pain."

All of us know from experience that the consequences of sin always include pain. When I sin, I hurt myself, others, and God. That's because sin:

- disrupts my relationship with God.
- disillusions the faith of others.
- damages the work of God.

No wonder God takes sin so seriously and works so diligently to help us become free! God, in His kindness, wants to spare all of us from the painful and destructive consequences of sin. That's why He will do everything in His power to keep us from evil—and to keep evil away from us and our loved ones.

Our friend Dianne recently learned this firsthand.

As you recall, Dianne's territory had expanded from teaching Bible studies to include speaking to large groups of women at retreats. "God was using my teaching in the lives of hundreds of women," she says. "It was amazing!" Another wonder was that even though her husband, Frank, isn't a Christian, he gave his support and even took care of the twins when she was on the road.

God, in His kindness, wants to spare all of us from the painful and destructive consequences of sin.

Then one morning, about a year after her first retreat, Dianne knew something had changed. As she prayed for her family, *Lord, keep us from evil,* she was immediately struck by the thought, *You need to be at home.*

"I couldn't understand it," she says. "God was blessing my ministry, and I loved teaching. Why couldn't I do both?"

For days Dianne struggled with the continuing urgency

in her heart. Finally, she tearfully surrendered to God her desire to teach women. She committed not to take any speaking engagements for at least the next six months.

That evening, Dianne shared her decision with her husband. After she finished, he remained silent. Finally, with Dianne's gentle prompting, Frank confessed to Dianne how difficult the past year had been on him and the boys. He told her that he'd been having problems at work and she never seemed to be around or available when he needed to talk.

Dianne looks back now and says, "I'm so overwhelmed by God's faithfulness!"

"But that wasn't all," she says. "When I heard what he said next, my heart froze." Frank went on to tell Dianne that a woman at work had been making advances toward him. Frank had remained loyal to Dianne physically, but he admitted that it had become increasingly hard to remain true to her in his thoughts.

Dianne was stunned by Frank's revelation. But that very night she and Frank began taking steps to restore their relationship. She looks back now and says, "I'm so overwhelmed by God's faithfulness! And I also saw how important my response was. What if I hadn't obeyed God's request to give up speaking and be at home?"

Over the next year Dianne and her husband worked on improving their marriage. Then one day Frank surprised Dianne by suggesting she resume some of her speaking. "I was amazed and very hesitant at first," Dianne says. "But eventually I understood. God hadn't been saying He didn't want me ever to minister to women, but just the opposite. He cared so much about expanding this part of my territory that He protected it. He halted it for a time so that I could later continue—with my priorities straight, my life in balance, and my husband's true blessing."

Dianne's story is a sobering reminder of how crafty Satan can be and how critical it is that we obey God. But it is also a reminder of just how diligently and faithfully God works in our lives to keep us from sin and its devastating consequences. Yes, you need to be alert to the enemy's schemes and then do your part in resisting temptation. But as the apostle John reminds us, "Greater is He who is in you than he who is in the world" (1 John 4:4, NASB).

The victory is ours when we pray, like Jabez, "Oh, that You would keep me from evil."

CHAPTER SIX

Never *the* Same

SO GOD GRANTED HIM
WHAT HE REQUESTED.

e're almost there!" My children heard my reassuring tone of voice, but after fifteen hours of driving, let's face it: "Almost there" isn't as good as being there!

So what about you? Are you "almost" convinced that the abundant life—the life you were made for—is only a prayer away? Or will you experience "being there" by choosing to pray the prayer of Jabez beginning today?

Every time we turn around, Bruce and I hear the same thing: "God has changed my life through the prayer of Jabez, and I will never be the same again!"

Why does this little prayer have such a positive effect on those who commit to sincerely pray it? Maybe it's because it leads us to discover what God has always known—we were made to live like this! What can possibly delight the heart of God more than to have His children ask for His blessing, seek to do more for Him, depend on His Spirit, and plead for His protection?

As a parent, you love to see your children fulfilled and content. It grieves you when they do just the opposite of what you've told them and the consequences bring pain. Why would we think our heavenly Father is any different?

As a parent, you love to see your children fulfilled and content.

Walking with God was meant to be the most exciting experience of life. And the prayer of Jabez takes us one step closer to turning what was meant to be into what is. So what could possibly hold you or anyone back from praying the Jabez prayer?

BREAKING THROUGH TO BLESSING

If you're still stranded at "almost there," maybe the following steps will help get you unstuck. If you're already "here," congratulations! These are still critical points for you to understand and to be able to pass on to others.

Determine to be persistent.

I remember the first time I prayed the Jabez prayer. Over the next few days, when nothing particularly exciting happened, I began to get discouraged. But then I asked myself something: *Do you always give your children what they want as soon as they ask you?*

I'm reminded of Chrissi and Dann, friends of mine who have a teenager named Krista. Sometimes when Krista comes to her parents and asks for something, they don't give her an immediate answer. They just say, "We'll see." Later, Chrissi and Dann discuss her request and decide what the answer will be. But even if it's yes, they don't always tell Krista right away.

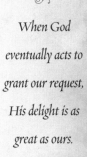

When God eventually acts to grant our request, His delight is as great as ours.

During the next few days, they listen to Krista share all the creative reasons why she thinks they should say yes. They enjoy watching her persistence and take pleasure in her sincere attempts to sway them. Often, it's a profitable process for all three of them as they discuss the pros and cons of granting her request. When they finally give Krista the yes she's been waiting for, her delight and excitement is far greater than if they had given her an immediate yes the first day.

I believe that God, as our heavenly Father, feels the same way. Even though He already knows our heart, He wants us to go through the process of persistently asking Him for what we desire. He knows that as we do this, we become convinced that what we are asking for is what He wants to give us. When He eventually acts to grant our request, His delight is as great as ours.

Remember that God's answers are individual.

The prayer of Jabez in its four parts will be the same for all of us:

- I will ask for and expect God's blessing on me.
- I will plead for more territory and respond to the opportunities when they come.
- I will depend upon God's hand to guide and direct me to accomplish what I could not do alone.
- I will ask God to keep evil away from me so that I will not bring grief to others, God, or myself.

However, the way God answers this prayer will never be the same for me as it is for you! It cannot be duplicated from one person's life to another. We will each experience entirely different answers with entirely different circumstances, with entirely different people, with entirely different lessons, with entirely different blessings.... You get the picture. This is not a group project.

It's so important to keep this in mind as you continue to pray this prayer and watch for God's answers. God may bless your good friend with a new van or a promotion at work. And if you miss this principle, you could end up somehow feeling less blessed. But the truth is that God blesses us and answers our prayers *perfectly*. He never makes mistakes or shortchanges His children. Every answer God gives us is intended to meet our unique needs and further God's purposes in our lives. God is transforming each of us individually. It is my personal relationship with God that is being affected. It is your personal relationship with God that is being affected…in different ways. Yet all for His glory!

The way God answers this prayer will never be the same for me as it is for you!

Make the prayer part of your family's lifestyle.

There's a lot of truth to the old saying "The family that prays together stays together." But guess what? The family that prays Jabez together not only stays together; it gets blessed together!

Even young children can understand the basic concepts of this little prayer. Break it down into simple ideas for them, such as, "God wants you to ask Him to give you good things"; "God wants you to have lots of friends and tell them all about Jesus"; "God wants to help you and make you strong for Him"; and "God wants to keep you away from bad things."

One mother I know asks her high school–age kids almost every night at dinner, "Did you have any Jabez Appointments today?" More often than not they have an exciting story to share.

Another way to make Jabez part of your family life is to pray the prayer on behalf of your family, friends, and church. One mother I know prays the prayer aloud for her children at night when she tucks them in, while yet another mom whispers the prayer every morning as her kids fly out of the house to catch the school bus. If you're like most women, you will vary the words from day to day and adapt them to fit unique situations as you pray for others. That's fine. No, that's wonderful!

Keep a record of your prayer journey.

It takes less than thirty seconds to pray the prayer of Jabez. But remember, this is a little prayer with big results. That's why I encourage you to do the following:

- Choose to pray the Jabez prayer every morning for thirty days and mark your calendar the day you begin so you can keep track of when you recognize God's first answer.
- Begin a notebook or journal to record the divine appointments God provides during your day. Just remember, those interruptions in your schedule may just be divine opportunities!
- Ask a friend to hold you accountable for the next

month to share what God is doing in your life through the prayer of Jabez.

A JABEZ LIFESTYLE

Over and over I've talked to women who tell me, "This is more than a prayer. It's a lifestyle."

What do they mean? They certainly don't mean that they worship Jabez instead of Jesus. I also don't think it means they wear Jabez necklaces or drink only from Jabez coffee cups. What they're saying is that praying the prayer of Jabez changes the way they think about God and life so dramatically that it affects their entire outlook on life on a daily basis.

God never makes mistakes or shortchanges His children.

And how could it not? When you pray, "Lord, bless me indeed!" you are reminded that God's nature is to bless, that He is a good and loving God.

When you pray, "Lord, expand my territory," you are reminded that you have a significant mission here on earth.

When you pray, "Lord, keep Your hand upon me," you are reminded that God's power is available in a supernatural way to you at every moment. Suddenly anything seems possible!

And finally, when you pray, "Keep me from evil, that I may not cause pain!" you are reminded that God has the power to protect you and that when you sin you hurt yourself, others, and God.

These are four simple but life-changing messages: God wants to bless me. God wants to use me. God wants to empower me. God wants to protect me. When we pray this way day after day, these truths become part of our consciousness and gradually begin to take hold and affect our actions. We begin to look for God's blessings. We begin to see people as potential ministry. We begin to seek God's power like never before, and because we don't want to break the cycle of God's blessing, we are more serious than ever about keeping evil and sin far from us.

God wants to bless me. God wants to use me. God wants to empower me. God wants to protect me.

May I encourage you to adopt a Jabez lifestyle? You've been standing on your tiptoes far too long. You were made for more than what you've been seeing up until now. Isn't it time to let God show you the big picture, the whole parade?

THE END OF THE STORY

Since we're near the end of this book, let's talk about the end of Jabez's story. Do you remember how it ended? "So God granted him what he requested" (1 Chronicles 4:10, NKJV).

Let me ask you something. If someone were telling your story at the end of your life, how would it read? Would it describe you as more honorable? Would it talk about how you prayed? How would it describe your lifestyle?

If you sincerely pray the prayer of Jabez on a regular basis and respond to God's hand in your life, there's one thing you can know for sure—and that's the *end* of your story. I have no doubt that it will read, "So God granted her what she requested."

But the end isn't here yet, is it? There's still so much to do, learn, and see. Life with God is an endlessly exciting adventure. And God doesn't want you to miss one moment of it. That's why He wants to hear your voice today, asking Him for His blessings and for a bigger view of all that's possible. It's time to enjoy the parade!

The publisher and author would love
to hear your comments about this book.

PLEASE CONTACT US AT:

www.multnomah.net/theprayerofjabez

The BreakThrough Series, Book One
The Prayer of Jabez™

#1 *New York Times* Bestseller

11 Million in Print!

- ISBN 1-57673-733-0
- 11 Million in Print!
- www.prayerofjabez.com
- www.jabezmillion.com
- 2001 Gold Medallion Book of the Year

The BreakThrough Series, Book Two
Secrets of the Vine™

#2 New York Times Bestseller

- ISBN 1-57673-975-9
- Over 3 Million in Print!
- www.secretsofthevine.com
- www.thebreakthroughseries.co